ANCIENT RHYTHMS

James G. Piatt

Printed and bound in the United States.

Contact the author or the publisher for permissions.

ISBN-10: 0985902833
ISBN-13: 978-0-9859028-3-4

Published by:

Broken Publications
PO Box 685
Eatonville, WA 98328

www.BrokenPublications.com

Edited & formatted for print & eBook by:

Jennifer-Crystal Johnson
www.JenniferCrystalJohnson.com

Book Cover art by Wallace Piatt
www.WallaceIsArt.com

James G. Piatt

Broken
Publications

A
Pacific Northwest
Publisher

www.BrokenPublications.com

Other Books by James G. Piatt:

The Monk, Broken Publications 2013
The Silent Pond, Broken Publications 2012
The Ideal Society, Cambridge Books 2012

Coming Soon:

The Nostradamus Prophecies

Table of Contents

Ancient Rhythms

Ancient Rhythms

The ghostly notes of an Indian flute ripple across
the face of the silent pond – the music pulls on
the rusted strings of an ancient lyre.
Hidden within the harmonious caves of
my lonely and nomadic heart, the soft melody
reverberates in my brain; it is an ancient
rhythm that calls to me and haunts the
essence of my past that resides in the depths,

the darkness of the night, with only remnants
of a waning moon glistening in the haze of
the misty night, the lingering howling of coyotes, and
the guttural voices of bull frogs croaking on the
sides of the stream. Beckoning long lost memories
that echo nostalgically in my soul, I walk
noiselessly upon brown pine needles strewn
upon a deer's path and listen to silence.

Listen… listen… listen to the silence,
listen quietly to the absence of the din of humanity,
allow the ancient voices singing inside your heart
to open your mind to lost reminiscences; let serenity
enter into the caverns of your mind like a dove fluttering
with a gentle softness into the safety of a huge, white-
barked Sycamore tree, where it can only be found
by those who love its soft cooing.

Do you hear it? Do you hear it? Notes from an
Indian flute echoing in your mind, an ancient,
melancholy rhythm bubbling up in the membranes
of your soul; it is that which was before you were, and
will be after you are no longer here. It reverberates
a cadence that beats like the pulsations of your heart, the
lovely notes reproducing images of what went before,
images of a calmer, more peaceful time, a time when
you were young and carefree.

Curative Rhythms

Tall barren Oaks
Rooted deeply
In dark earth,
Entombed
Amid twisted
Umber-colored Birches,
Sending pleas that reach high
To the heavens with
Deciduous prayers that
Sway in the
Whispering breezes,
Chanting life's curative
Rhythms, softly calming
Yearning souls.

The Night Frog

The frog croaks its lonely sound in the moonlight;
It weeps multihued notes into my sleeping ears.
It sends me guttural poems and haunting tales of yore.
It is an earthy, pious droning that sinks into the dark
      soil.
It is united with all that breathes and pushes my mind
Into the earth until it tastes humanity.
I long to see that warty frog that sings such songs, but
It has passed unseen into the darkness of its own
      melody.

Moonlight Sonata

I listened to Mozart being played by my
love on the old Spinet; the melody drifted through
the evening's gentle atmosphere like a poem.
I closed my eyes and watched our memories
drift on top of black and white notes.

I am now alone, and as I gaze out the window
by the old Spinet, I see the Evening Star,
the eyelet of heaven's shade, pulling
gray down into vivid pink, then
watch as dusk vanishes into darkness.

I am now a solitary one in the velvety
darkness of a lonely night. With only the
glimmering stars to light my way, I drift
into the past, with memories of my love playing
the Sonata in my aging mind, and I softly weep.

The Glass Pond

The opalescent, soundless pond,
like smooth glass, rests peacefully
inside my morning thoughts,

the downy breath of serenity floating
atop soft currents of summer's heated
voice, opens happy memories in my heart.

The Ring-Necked Dove

I glimpse a ring-necked dove
perched on the limb of a
Sycamore tree; it coos
its mating song.
Like a child,
I listen to its poem
of love aimlessly
crawling into my soul.
While my mind laughs,
I realize
the simplicity of its being
contains answers
without excuses.

Sleep Calmly, My Child

Sleep calmly, my child,
while the journey
of the day ends.
Leave today's problems
with yesterday's lost memories, for
upon the golden morn,
a new day will come.

The night is peaceful;
be in oneness
with the glittering stars
puncturing
the velvety darkness,
for they
will comfort you.

Sleep calmly, my child,
without cares, and
allow your dreams
to wander,
for in them
you will find
the peace you deserve
so dearly!

Precious Times

Sitting on the rocky edge
of a flowing stream, I
listen to the rhythm
of a tree that sings and
rooks that quote gaudy poems
on unearthly strings.
The sun above beams its warmth
onto a green-clad knoll
as crickets play gaudy poems
on slender legs into
my lonely soul;
I remember those younger times
since my birth, and
try not to forget the time given
to me was precious, and
at times… quite droll!

Things We Forget

In the rush to gain material things, our soul becomes lost.

We forget the beauty

Of a forest filled with giant red trees stretching to heaven,
And the lacy green fern beneath them; a small
Blue tarn resting peacefully inside a mountain vale,
surrounded
With white-barked Aspens; Giant Sycamore trees that try to
touch
The welcoming sky above their extended limbs.

We forget the beauty of

Small brown and black chipmunks scurrying about for acorns,
Regal hawks soaring majestically in the sapphire sky, rainbow
trout
Leaping for gnats in clear mountain streams, tiny fat pollywogs
wiggling
Happily in small rills, white-capped mountains, and meadows
Of green and yellow; Translucent, salty blue-green waves
In a beaconing teal ocean, multicolored wildflowers of
Blue, pink, and red, bluebirds - robins - woodpeckers and gray
quail.

We forget the beauty of

Small hidden glens tucked between brown and purple
Mountainous chasms, forming deep verdant dells;
White, yellow, and blue butterflies flitting about in hidden
Groves; Spider webs glistening with diamonds of
Morning dew, and blue birds in a vocal performance
High in nearby trees.

We forget the beauty of

Small brooks laden with colored wood frogs, silver Carp,
Innocent, smiling children giggling as they romp in
Shallow pools, and white-haired grandfathers
Wearing old tilted baseball caps, with lopsided
Smiles on their lips and a gleam in their aging eyes!

The Mockingbird

Oh mockingbird, ignoble feathered beast
of the midnight hours, with multiple
voices trilling stridently in the moonlit
night. You are as a lost soul, calling for
your mate in solo flight! You must be
listening to the wandering moon, for
anon the dawn will rise, and
like someone led astray in the fallow
meadows of the day, only gray embers
of your wishful memories will stay.
Ennobled by Eros' sting, your gaudy
notes will, as the night rises, once again sing.

One Evening

Serene the evening without the city's din,
A night of peace without scarred asphalt:

The winds, calm – silent, skimmed the earth
And kissed the sides of the smooth shore,

The pond's skin smooth as new blown glass,
With gaudy birds digging in its sandy edges:

The stars fixed with a gleaming gaze
Shone brightly upon the steadfast two;

They sat among the precious silence
And stared at the glimmering orb above,

With speech low, she wooed her lover,
He held her tightly so time would cease.

Inside the Apse

I love hours spent inside
a sunlit apse, where
prayer candles light
the way to forgiveness
amid a tinted misty haze.

I feel currents of infinite love,
beaconing from the nave as
they envelop my drifting soul.

In this ancient church, wearing
a headdress of ancient spires,
my mind dances gaily in its
halls of towering carved arches.

I love the blue and gold painted
images, staining panels
of sacred windows, seemingly
swaying gaily like tiny Cherubs.

I love the haunting chanting of
the voices of Benedictine Monks as
they drift down, down, down
to our scarlet souls below,
their ancient songs coiling around my
essence, bringing a silent calmness.

A pious bumblebee mumbling in its
perfumed existence flits about
in my soul and exalts in
prayerful answers to my
childish human prayers, as I
kneel down on an oaken pew in
the stillness of a sunny
afternoon.

I Calmly Wend My Carefree Way

Amid confusion of wealth seeking guise,
Among men with power in their eyes,
I care not, for amongst all their cliché,
I calmly wend my carefree way.

They purchase jewels to tease other men,
They toil each day to plunder them, and
Waste their time to utter dismay, but
I calmly wend my carefree way.

The verdant woods and wild flowers are mine,
The blue heavens and the poet's rhyme,
And amidst the calm of a peaceful lea,
I calmly wend my carefree way.

The Evening's Soft Glow

In the softness of the evening's glow
as the ocean tide arrives in cerulean blue,
I marvel at the gleaming stars above so true
as they gleam upon we poor souls below.
The sea's current brings in things so slow,
like a ship's broken wheel and an old shoe,
while the warm sands and the winds eschew.
Then when, at dusk, time moves so very slow,
my soul exalts in the gentle peace, and
within my mind happy memories grow as
dark thoughts are quickly washed away.
As depressing feelings begin to decrease,
a warm mist of serenity comes to stay and
sad misgivings begin to go.

His Healing Balm

He whispers in the ears of those who dream,
Touches hearts to transform wandering souls,

For those who listen, He sends a singing stream,
For those who read He gives His sacred scrolls,

He covers all sins with his crimson dust,
Grants all humanity His forgiving love,

Weeps over those who cannot adjust, and
Forgives all sins, with the silence of a dove,

In the early morning when thoughts are clear,
He grants all absolution and a peaceful calm, and

Wonders why men are still filled with fear, and
Refuse to feel the coolness of his healing balm.

My Serenity

Melancholy thoughts of aging summer
Give flight as gentle rains of autumn
Rinse away the dust from Spanish moss
Clinging like urchins to shadowy oaks
Dotting the soil in verdant pastures

Sweet vestiges of private dreams
Narrow blades of worry vanishing
Slipping away covered in white mist
Leaving only golden gilded memories
Of glimmering and serene sensations

Woven strings of recollections
Merge with cloudy cool evenings
Next to glowing fires in hearth
Easy conversations of braided delight
Flow contentedly in peaceful minds

Summer Has Arrived

Visions of warm days have come to stay;
The ocean's blue tide is calm and still,
the warm breath of summer does easily flow.

Frozen streams and barren trees no longer dismay;
My summer heart is now lightened and still –
visions of warm days have come to stay.

Warm dreams arrive as winter nightmares decay,
the mountains no longer white with winter's chill;
The warm breath of summer does easily flow.

Unfriendly spring winds, no longer cold or gray,
blurring the warm sun to the iceman's will;
Visions of warm days have come to stay.

Friendly breezes of summer are due again today,
blowing warm thoughts into our pleasant hill;
The warm breath of summer does easily flow.

In months ahead, warm winds will remain so gay,
for visions of warm days have come to stay, and
countless sunny rays will reflect upon the rill, while
the warm breath of summer does easily flow.

A Special Summer Day

Cherry-tipped clouds painted in the sky,
far atop small, verdant glades hidden below.
We travel on twisted patchwork roads on high
into ancient quilts of green where flowers grow.
Umber-colored oaks, soft green pines,
pinecones strewn like dark brown jewels,
warm, soft winds, hot sun, cool red vines, and
stately trees cover blue, tranquil pools.
When our souls breathe in so deeply,
sitting atop pine needles so brown,
a quiet serenity covers us so steeply
as the translucent water flows, up and down;
The slow-moving river carries us to
peaceful dreams
under evening stars.

Warm, Soft Summer Winds

Warm soft summer winds
Hot sun
Brown and gnarled bark
Above verdant peaks
Aromas of musty pines
Enveloped me with gentle shadows
Inner vibrations
Covered with a soft silver mist
Calm my anxious mind

Warm Night Breezes

Warm night breezes,
Carrying the aromas of musty
Pine into the air,
Lingering in my senses,
Giving birth to peacefulness.

The Iron Horse traveling on
Ancient iron rails, escapes
Into the distance, and with a
A lingering haunting sound,
Carries my dreams into
The night.

Time Passes Too Quickly

Pine needles crunching under sensitive feet,
Red boulders sprouting from cold water in
A shallow pool: glassy water and green moss,
A slight breeze. Flies buzzing through
The stillness of gentle thoughts, rugged
Mountains erupting into the blue sky,
Frogs croaking in the dark shadows of
Broken shale.
I am alone, but not lonely.
A sudden silence brings an
Awareness of the soft, finite time
Of our lives that passes too quickly.

The Placid Pond

Silver, soundless,
The placid pond
Rests peacefully
Inside a meadow's
Verdant glen.

A downy dove
Atop soft currents of
A warm summer's
Breeze coos into
The gentleness of the
Air, sending soft
Healing rhythms into
My aching heart.

Thoughts on the Beach

Sea jewels sparkling beneath
The foam of incoming tides
Precious thoughts beguiling and
Mystifying us by hiding
Under tiny rivulets of brine

Colored seashells, bits of conscience
Beckon to all those who ride in on the
Gawky undercurrents of
Gaudy hidden
Scarlet longings

Sand blowing upon sand
Forever shifting with gusty winds
Gritty desires
Pull us into steep perspectives
Of our morality and
Leave us graceless

The Ocean's Tide

Spring's afternoon sun
Warms my wandering soul,
Sea gulls and terns cry
Loudly over the muted
Voices of sand dunes, so
Smooth, so delicate, while
      The ocean's tide comes and goes

The sun peeks quietly
Over sheer cliffs, as the sea
Hides in tidal shadows;
White-topped waves burrow with
White talons into the ocean's
Sandy shore, while
      The ocean's tide comes and goes

The late afternoon arrives,
Heaven's orb dips to the horizon,
Bathers leave with shell tokens, and
When their happy laughter is
Only a fading memory,
Sea creatures come ashore and
      The ocean's tide comes and goes

The Briny Sea

The ocean's tide
Comes and goes, and

Barbed steps in the sand
Show barren toes;

Toward the dark sea
They mutely point,

To a dark scene that
Will sadly disappoint,

Someone is leaving
This earth in a silent repose,

A life too fragile to be
Will soon dispose, and

In a minute, will forlornly
Return to the briny sea.

James G. Piatt

Time By a Lazy Flowing Brook

I love the hours spent beside a lazy flowing brook
Covering the verdant ground with its misty blue haze.
A warm autumn stillness covers my wandering soul, as
My mind dances in the halls of ancient memories.
I love the green painted leaves hanging from
The smooth white-barked Sycamore trees,
Swaying gaily in the wind like tiny dancing gypsies.
I love to listen to the soft chanting of the
Gurgling brook as it curls its way down,
Down, down to the beckoning lake below.
The brook's drenched song coils around my thoughts,
Bringing a soft quietness, while the bumblebee
Mumbling softly in its perfumed existence
Flits about in my mind as I wander in my own
Circular pattern of yesterday's dreams.

A Wintry Rill

A wintry rill
surges
through
meadows
and strands,
like a
baffling
reflection
knitting a
forlorn
dream. In its
wake, I see
images of a
mystifying
scheme
pushing
deeply into
white and
frozen lands,
where Birch
trees become
barren by
winter's icy
hands.
Flowers
alongside a
quick-
flowing
stream,
where
downed
trunks and
boulders
with varied
seam, form
wintry

walkways
for my cold
winter plans.
My rootless
mind dares
not complain,
for winter's
white
images one
cannot
forsake, for a
white
calmness will
royally reign,
and in the
midst of a
soaring,
dreamlike
state, tall
gray clouds
will release a
refreshing
rain, and as I
tread a
snowy path,
in a wintry
stillness I
will partake.

Winter at the Farm

Icy winds blow
Long strings of
Frozen rain,
Draped like
A wedding gown,
Dazzling white
Upon a crooked fence.
Twisted flowers
From aged pepper trees,
Beautifully tossed
Pale pink jewels
Upon ecru grass,
Warm fire inside a
Brick fireplace,
Keeping bodies restful and
Minds serene….

January Days

Brisk cold winds blowing
Through barren birch trees
Chanting wintry tunes through my mind
They beget a cold apprehension

Sandstone boulders emerging
From a cold, tumultuous pool
Forming poignant doubts in my dreams
Detached and distant thoughts emerge

Echoes of the winter wind
Rippling through whispered silence
Stirring uneasiness in my body
And a sad melancholy in my mind

Cold lingering murmurings
Echoing down steep, rocky trails
Carried by intense, gusty winds
Piercing the serenity of my existence

Mammoth pieces of dark granite
Reaching toward ghostly skies
Painting shadows in my mind
Restlessness fills my being

I long for the golden sun
And the rays of balmy zephyrs
The melody of soft moving streams and
Smooth, warm afternoons

Winter is Here

Sweet visions of warm shores are fading away,
the ocean's tide no longer calm and still –
the icy breath of winter is reflected in snow.

Frozen streams and barren trees dismay,
my summer heart is abandoned and shrill;
sweet visions of warm shores are fading away.

Cold thoughts linger as sunny dreams decay,
the mountains white with winter's chill;
the icy breath of winter is reflected in snow.

The unfriendly winds blow icy and gray,
turning the sun to the iceman's will –
sweet visions of warm shores are fading away.

Unfriendly gusts of winter are due again today,
blowing warm thoughts far away from the hill;
the icy breath of winter is reflected in snow.

In the months ahead, the cold wind will go away and
sunnier days will reflect upon a rill, but for now,
sweet visions of warm shores are fading away and
the icy breath of winter is reflected in snow.

The Fading Winter

Today, the season of sparrows chirping
In the budding white birch trees
While doves coo to their mates begins

A time for the quickening in things
As the burgeoning sun glows less dimly
At its higher angle of bright repose

A time for less vigorous fires in the hearth
Where colorful oak embers of red and yellow
Once sent outward warmth to chilled bodies

Who can deny the hope of the final white dew
Upon a rusted barbed wire fence in the chilled morn
Or swaths of pale green appearing in the hills

Leggy roses with brand new buds appearing
Tell the infinite tale of the cycle of death and
Birth upon the warm and darkened earth

Now in my orchard garden of fading winter
Tiny shoots begin to emerge softly
Among the garrulous and spiteful weeds

Behind my crumbling rock wall hides
The beginnings of new hollyhocks
Waiting for sunnier days to bloom

Resignedly under gray clouded skies
Spring strives ever boldly to lose the
Winter melancholy driven into the earth

I feel the swelling of pendulous breezes
Creeping into new, luminous thoughts
Bringing renewed waves of happy anticipation

Ancient Rhythms

Winter is leaving and sere leaves of brown
Are being replaced with tiny green buds, and
My lighter heart sings hymns of bliss

Soon the weeding and planting begins
And the gardens will begin to blossom
Here is to the fading of winter

'Tis Spring Again

'Tis spring and it's balmy and serene;
colorful birds soar ever so still and
a warm sun envelops the land.

In verdant meadows now painted green,
the tree frogs' voices sing happy and shrill:
'tis spring and it's balmy and serene!

Spring always so lovely to behold, the
brooks are transparent and sunny is the hill;
a warm sun envelops the land.

I long for more things to quickly unfold,
like the gentle flowing of a tiny rill;
'tis spring and it's balmy and serene.

I enjoy the beauty of flowers that unfold,
I smile daily that there is no icy chill;
a warm sun envelops the land.

A gentle serenity is foretold, and
to the warmth of the sun I do thrill;
'tis spring and it's balmy and serene, and
a warm sun envelops the land.

Spring's Meadows

Quilts of green under trees
Once inert and fallow,
Gleaming coral beads
Hanging from a pepper tree

Tiny wrens fluttering amidst
Brisk, balmy spring winds,
Gray squirrels retrieving acorns
From dark, hidden hollows

Giant Cumulous clouds,
Fluffs of white cotton
Overflowing with moisture,
Sweeping across mountains

Writing sentences in white
About the coming spring,
Verdant fields of fresh color, and
Meadows laden with newness!

Images of Spring

Visions of balmy days are coming this way
The tide no longer cold, churning, and shrill
The warm breath of spring does easily flow

Slow flowing streams and leafy trees do sway
Hearts are filled with spring's gentle will
Visions of balmy days are coming this way

Spring arrives quickly as winter fades away
The mountains no longer white with winter's quill
The warm breath of spring does easily flow

The clouds no longer cold and gray
Blurring the dulling sun to the iceman's will
Visions of balmy days are coming this way

Balmy spring breezes are due again today
Blowing serene thoughts into our pleasant hill
The warm breath of spring does easily flow

White hills are no longer ready for the sleigh
For visions of balmy days are coming this way
No more winter storms bluster upon the rill, and
The warm breath of spring does easily flow

Coming of Spring

I sit by a gentle, flowing stream,
playing an ancient Indian flute;
clear blue water flows slowly
across smooth pebbles
of green, brown, and white – God's
sculptures of translucent gypsum.

I listen to the soft rustling
of singing Sycamore leaves
in a verdant butte far away;
I marvel at a pin-tailed deer
as it leaps in sheer delight
at its unlimited freedom.

I listen to the soft cooing of
a covey of California quail
as the wind blows softly through
white- and gray-barked Birch trees
hugging the sides of a meandering rill.

I gaze at the soft blue sky,
with delicate white clouds
moving so lacy and frail;
the sun's gentle rays caress
my shoulders, warming them.

I squeeze the soft, smooth pebbles
beneath my toes and watch silently
as countless speckled rainbow trout
swim lazily down the flowing stream
to safer havens in the yellow sand.

I am away from common trials
and stressful human demands,
but within my searching soul
I feel the world's loneliness, and
tears flow swiftly down my cheeks.

A Spring Brook

A spring brook meanders through meadows and strands,
like some unsolved thought weaving a lost theme while
creating colorful visions of a spring-wrapped dream.
It pushes deeply into colorful, flowered lands, amidst
Sycamore trees green with spring's dampened hands.
Flowers flourish alongside the flowing stream, where
downed trunks and boulders with varied seams
form fresh walkways for my future summer plans.
My wandering and aging mind does not complain, and
the spring's windy vagaries I do not forsake,
for a balmy peacefulness doth royally reign, and
in the midst of this lofty, dreamlike state,
soft, billowy clouds above I do not deign, for
smiling to myself, a serenity I do partake.

Spring Time

The residue of winter nights wither away, and
Warmth enters with a serene spring morn:
Memories of frigid days no longer shrill.

The gloomy remnants of winter gales sway,
Warm spring winds in the knoll are born:
Remnants of winter nights wither away.

Happy thoughts of spring are born today,
Winter's cold darkness blown and torn:
Memories of frigid days no longer shrill.

Warmth of a yellow rising sun will stay,
Past icy memories will no longer forlorn:
Remnants of winter nights wither away.

I greet the heat of the sun's royal ray
Into my longing heart, it flows un-torn:
Memories of frigid days no longer shrill.

No icy bits of darkness can again dismay
In this place where true love is unworn,
The remnants of winter nights wither away,
Memories of frigid days no longer shrill.

Spring

Silver, soundless,
my soul's memories
rise up in hope,
like the blue-green
rapids of a slow-
moving stream,
like a downy dove
atop currents of a
warm spring breeze.
Delicate, fluttering leaves
gleaming on Sycamore trees
calm my anxious thoughts,
nature's healing symphony
sings in my longing soul as
verdant reeds with
furry, brown tops
sway in a balmy wind.
The wrinkled skin
of a lazy pond ripples
in glee as my
troubled thoughts
are covered
with contented illusions,
scattering my fears afar.

Spring Love

After rasping winds abated,
after winter departed and
gray clouds loosened
their sorrowful woes
in mountain streams,
like old men releasing
fears of aging—

Spring seeds, carelessly
strewn by gaudy birds
upon the earthen face
of the glade near
spring's entrance,
blossomed and
perfumed the verdant
valley with sweetness.

White, billowing clouds
swirled blissfully
atop fertile mountains,
craggy and steep, and
young lovers' hearts
chimed in unison with
nature's emerging newness.

Images of castles and
princes floating
amid towering clouds
gliding beneath
the warming sun,
impassioned, young
lovers' hearts—

Amidst soft moss, they
frolicked happily,
following the way
of all young lovers
in spring's golden glow,
alive with passions
of youthful gaiety,
amorous in
Eve's garden of
delight.

Spring at the Farm

New sprouts;
Beginning of life:
Rose buds,
White, red, pink, green.
Herb sprouts
Pushing up from
Deep, rich soil:
Rich earth
Anxious to emit
Nourishment.
Fruit trees,
Green, pink blossoms;
Beautiful elderly woman
On her hands
And knees,
Gently sifting
Humid earth,
Like she has done
For so many seasons,
So peaceful
In her garden of
Tasty delights.

Oh Balmy Breeze

Oh balmy breeze, you are the breath of spring,
You from whom newness comes each day,
A presence that brings new life to our being,
A bouquet of colors blowing away the gray

Oh balmy breeze, you are the heart of life, a
Welcoming freshness which overcomes the night,
You bring brightness to overcome our strife, and
Toll in soft bells that cover dark winter's blight

Oh balmy breeze, you are the hope of warmer days,
You bring in the verdant meadows for us to view,
So sweet your rhythm over life's pleasant ways,
You are a sweet song that echoes in my soul so true

A Spring Day

I love to sit by a rushing stream

Playing my Indian flute and watching
Clear blue water cascading
Frantically across smooth stones of
Brown, black, and white

I love to hear the rasping rustle

Of Sycamore leaves
In a nearby butte, while
Marveling at a pin-tailed doe
Leaping in sheer delight

I love to eavesdrop on a soft cooing

Covey of gray quail,
As spring winds bluster
Through white-barked Birches
And ancient Oaks

I love to gaze at hazy blue skies

With delicate white clouds
So frail, filled with moisture, as
The sun's rays caress the soil
Making it warm

I love to stroke cool pebbles

Beneath my toes, and
Watch silently as speckled
Trout swim down the stream

Mostly, I thank God I am far away
From the stressful sights and sounds
Of the weary world!

Essence of Nature

The sage's words too harsh
The poet's words don't rhyme
The artist's canvas too sparse
The architect's lines too sublime

Nature's beauty beyond inscription
Inner secrets impossible to learn
Her harsh innocence defies description
Her pure simplicity too deep to discern

My Soul Flows

In the presence of
serenity,
my essence soars
cheerfully,
like the autumn wind
amidst tall Pines,
like an angel
emptying
joyful thoughts into
a drifting
soul.

One Lovely, Pleasant Night

'Tis a lovely, pleasant night – so serene, so still,
Blessed and calm as a church's hallowed cell.
The candle's soft rays cast their holy spell and
Warm my heart from the winter's frosty chill.
Downy birds sing gaily nearby in a hidden rill;
My heart rejoices, and my fears they quell, as
Their singing voices in my soul softly dwell, and
In my mind, melodious echoes gently trill.
Her soft hand in mine I tenderly grasp, and
Holding my breath, I kiss her yielding lips, and
With pulse beating wildly, I hold her near, and
Give her a velvet box with a carved golden hasp,
Solemnly promising her mansions and grand trips,
Swearing her life will never be dull or austere.

When the Evenings Are

When the evenings are spacious and yellow
and the spring flowers have shrunken and folded,
you can – if you close your human eyes – see
that beauty still exists in the sweet scent.

The ocean's foam is still found in blue slowness
and young men's hopes in women's folly;
the fairest of flowers are forever those
still in seed and in the bud's dew.

Promise me light when the moon wanes,
grant me tiny beams shining in glory;
do not weary my mind with darkness,
only illuminate it with all that is beautiful.

Do not tease me with false visions of hope,
or saddened visions of dark, fathomless seas.
Bring me to calm, clear streams and warm sand, and
place my head in your welcoming lap.

James G. Piatt

In the Beauty of the Evening

In the vast beauty of the evening glow,
The foamy tide arrives a sapphire blue.

I marvel at myriad stars so true
As they shimmer upon we souls below.

The current brings things with a soft blow,
Like brown kelp and an old tennis shoe.

The warm sand the gusty winds eschew,
In the dusk where time moves so slow.

Dark thoughts are washed away and
Serene feelings begin to increase.

My mind exalts in a gentle peace, and
Within my thoughts, new memories grow

As serenity slowly comes to stay and
Shadowy misgivings begin to go.

Searching

In my search for sacred phrases,
I came upon an ancient scheme which
Disturbed my calm and tranquil ways.
I tried to conceal it in a peaceful theme,
Smother it under a joyful haze, but
When it persisted like a raucous dream,
I concealed my fears in a poetic maze.

I try to remain serene near a peaceful stream
When confronted with thoughts I find so dim,
But I sadly find myself despising those
Terrible things I find so dark and grim.
I then fill my mind with things surprising,
And in my amused delight I find it brings
Peaceful rhymes, upon angel's wings.

In Love's Sweet Garden

In love's sweet garden, our affection will grow
among the roses, violets, and pansies low.
In the soft, warm soil of our shared affection,
amid our evening dreams of soft perfection,
we will live and love under cerulean sky.

Where wrens and hummingbirds softly fly,
negative thoughts will be strewn awry,
gaudy bird-like memoirs will become confection;
in love's sweet garden, our affection will grow.

Pleasant kisses and a shared caress,
lovingly shared without excess,
with soft touches and words of love,
will be a beam of light to all above
and a true reminder to those below;
in love's sweet garden, affection will grow.

Love Continues

Boyish blond hair
Graying and thin
Once strong fingers
Now bony and frail
A heart crying out
To the child within
A soul trying to recall
A vanishing tale
A mind seeking
For answers to life
A soul searching
For reasons to be
Weary hands reaching
For his loving wife
Lean arms encircling
Her thin body
Sitting together
Her head on his chest
The best of life
Still in their grasp
His wife gives him
A loving embrace
Their love still an
Unbreakable clasp

Love

Feelings combine within
The mute caverns of my soul,
Hidden from anxious minds

Tiny bits of dark misgivings,
Like brown and gnarled bark,
Burn and the pain slowly departs

Amid the peaceful embers,
The warm stillness emits
Your love's soothing passion

To all of those who truly love,
The perfect combination of songs
Are found in the rhythm of the heart

I now listen not to mere words,
But to the soft, gentle murmurings
Springing from your devoted heart

Gentle feelings of love reside there,
Tender images emerge and combine
Then flow like soft, warm breezes

The soft murmurings of your love
Hidden inside your heart sing softly
To the longings in my lonely soul

Let Us Forget

Let us forget

War, and
instead, listen to the guttural
croaking of frogs in a pond
when the moon is high and
we are safely tucked in our beds.

Let us forget

Dissention, and
instead, listen to the soft murmuring
of ring-necked doves cooing in the
dew of the early morn as we stroll
atop pine needles on a country path.

Let us forget

Death, and
instead, listen to promises of
gentle prayers wafting through
tall pines in the balmy evening while
we swing together on our
old wooden swing.

James G. Piatt

Together Our Love Grows Strong

Dead fallow fields often do dismay,
flowers can wither and go astray, but
amidst the wintry days with their illusion,
my love for you is without confusion and
our times together will always be gay.

When dreams are hollow and go away,
when another's love lasts but a mere day,
when solemn oaths become delusions,
together our love grows strong.

In times of stress when love doth fray,
our love for each other will never stray;
in months and years with dark intrusions,
we will continue to love without allusion, and
our love will always be like a scented bouquet;
together our love grows strong.

The Sun So Bright Covers the Land

'Tis summer and west winds are warm and bold;
Colorful, downy birds glide ever so still, and
The sun so bright covers the land.

In flowered meadows now painted gold,
The mottled frogs' voices sing loud and shrill…
'Tis summer and west winds are warm and bold.

Summer always so beautiful to behold,
The brooks are clear and sunny is the hill…
The sun so bright covers the land.

I long for more time to hastily unfold,
Like the gentle flowing of a tiny rill;
'Tis summer and west winds are warm and bold

I enjoy the beauty of the flowers that unfold,
I smile daily that there is no icy chill, as
The sun so bright covers the land.

The warmth of summer has foretold, and
To the warmth of the sun I do thrill;
'Tis summer and west winds are warm and bold, as
The sun so bright covers the land.

You and Me

Let's find a place where birds can soar
And butterflies hang in glittering droves
Let's leave together to some ocean shore
And feel warm sand between our toes

Let's dream and wish for a precious time
And sit and hold each other's hands
Let's walk among tall trees that chime
Far away from cold white lands

Let's sit quietly amid a tall Pine grove
And watch squirrels flit from tree to tree
Let's share timeless love in a hidden cove
Hoarding precious moments, just you and me

A Peaceful Stillness

Lonely thoughts ascend
like eagles into the sky,
soaring in strident winds
amidst tall trees in a glade,
pouring forth dark memories
which the murmuring of
longing souls cannot deny.
The thoughts increase in
riotous turmoil atop wandering
currents in the forlorn caverns
of hopelessness, exploding
into crimson dust,
despair destroys happiness
without compassion.
Listen not to the lonely
cries of doom exploding like
splintered glass, causing
hollow tears to fall
like dead leaves in a forest;
heed only sounds of hope,
they will create a peaceful
stillness in your aching
soul.

Figueroa Mountain

Ancient patchwork quilt of
Gray and black asphalt bursts
Into a soft pale green mist of
Stately pines amidst umber
Painted gnarled ancient Oaks

Zephyrus voices sing softly
To the center of my weary soul
Orange-tipped clouds of dawn appear
And smells of musty wild berries
Infuse pleasantly into my senses

Quiet serenity slowly envelops me
Like delicate pine needles gently
Strewn upon my mind's path
Hard currents of dark thoughts
Disappear into humming breezes

A small, verdant dell covered
With wandering deer paths
Sounds of birds wafting through
Pine-scented breezes whisper
To my soul, drifting upon soft currents

Here my footfalls lead to ancient
Streams pulsating with healing music
Life's dark confusing dreams
Disappear into a soothing peace
Under soft silver-blue skies

Visage Beatha

After the break of day,
after stormy gales
among fallow leas,
white with winter's breath and
hidden in cold dells
between brown hills,
snow flowers
blowing in icy winds
waft their lovely scent.
Ripples in swiftly
flowing brooks,
searching, gurgling,
dashing over
granite rocks,
gaily laugh at the
season's yearning breath,
becoming a liquid procession of
the water of life!

Pleasant Memories

Pleasant memories have come to stay
My mind is silent and peacefully still
They live in my happy dreams at night

In colorful shards of glass so gay
The final echoes spew peacefully and still
Pleasant memories have come to stay

In the blissful sunlight of the day
They sing within a boisterous rill
They live in my happy dreams at night

Serene thoughts are those that stay
Around the window's flowered sill
Pleasant memories have come to stay

And in the stillness of my aging way
These thoughts overcome evil's will
They live in my happy dreams at night

In the tranquil images formed as I pray
In my searching mind, thoughts instill
Pleasant memories have come to stay
They live in my happy dreams at night

Music's Power

On an ancient mahogany spinet, as her thin fingers
Deftly play glorious and intricate combinations of sounds,
The sweet aroma of Beethoven lingers in the atmosphere
Of the room. My tears celebrate his poignant music, my
Joy commemorates his genius.

The notes of the first movement
Of the beautiful Moonlight Sonata
Echo off the walls like tiny black dancing elves;
My ears hunger for the magical notes to
Send a message of truth into my longing spirit.

New sensations emerge, while chords
Reverberate deeply in my brain. I feel
A peculiar and soothing calm, listening
To his beautiful, mysterious, and
Haunting music.

As I sit and listen to the chords drifting upon my
Ears from the ancient spinet, I sense the notes
Drifting intensely into my soul…. That is when I
Fully realized the awesome power of music, a
Power to transcend and reform.

The poignant music brought forth from her fingers
Upon the black and white keys evoked in my
Mind the sweet fragrance of forgotten memories,
The awareness of eternity, and an illumination
To answers to mankind's enigmas.

In music, there is no deception, it induces truth and
Happiness in its wake and traces of magic are
Found everywhere in its melodies. Music affects
Everything and touches everyone. Music lingers
In the mind long after the notes fade away.

It was then that I realized that music and
Love were one and the same, music and
Prayers were symbiotic, and music and
Memories were tied together inside notes, and
All were united together within chords.

I recognize now that notes played upon an instrument
Are the only hope that man has to bring forth a
Mutual understanding of the necessity for communal
Oneness. I also realize that the only way to world peace
Is through music, and that if music disappears, so will the
world.

Vanishing Summer Sun

Winter comes and ice fills the streets;
I hear the squishing of tires in
Opaque pools and
Long for summer's warmth, and
Feel a sudden coldness in
My aging bones...
Let me linger for a while
In the reminiscences of summer time;
Let me bide my time for just a while
In the serenity of a lazy flowing stream,
Let me remain for just a moment
As the ocean's current
Draws closer to shore…
Oh wretched body, so tired, so weary,
Cease your aches and cares,
Follow your youthful mind
That can still hear
The gentle buzzing of bees in a
Colorful garden…
Oh wretched fading mind, listen
Closely to the songs of gaudy birds
In tall trees, keep awake so
My soul can recall for a time
The vanishing summer sun!

She is Gone

A presence suddenly felt,
A gentle kiss upon his cheek,
He wavers, knowing it is
Only a soft breeze
Upon his damp face…
A new tear falls softly.

Looking into the mirror,
He sees an old man's face —
Had he aged so much
Since she went away?
He still felt so young
When he thought of her.

Her existence lingers
In his aging mind
Every hour of each day,
Sweet perfume of dreams
Keeps him living
Until the dark comes.

Night brings lonely hours
And sleepless longings…
Not until the sunny morn comes
Do the dark thoughts vanish;
Not until the light comes
Does he live again.

Life

You are a jealous mistress,
Covered wordlessly
In your silken veil

You are miserly,
Allowing too few
Years of happiness

You are too complex
For simple folk
And dreamers

You give too little,
Take too much
To partake in fullness;
You are too long
For those who live
In physical or mental pain

You are too short
For those who live
In serenity and love

What would we do
Without your boundless
Gifts of timeless possibilities

The Poem

A poem should be truthful
Yet vague,
Like an old left shoe;
Silent,
Yet noisy as a brass band,
It should be verbose, but
With few words, and
Unlike the sun
With its overt existence,
It should be false as a mask,
Yet, true as grief,
Like a lantern in the night,
Yet dimly lit,
It should not enlighten—
It should only exist
So lovers' minds can
Decipher the coded words
With their souls!

On a Mountain Top

The whispering of gentle winds
Twisting gracefully among white Birch
A white Egret standing on one leg
Eying a lazy green frog sitting on a pad
Muted echoes of a hidden brook in
A verdant dell far down the hill
The gentle peace of a serene mountain
Cradled by feathery white clouds
Veiled from all the world's anxiety
My love's long, auburn hair
Graying gracefully in finite time
Peaceful hours thinking of her
And writing her special rhyme

A World to Mold

On a soft and sunny afternoon, writing
Words that give me wistful solace,
I look up at the bright sun peeking through
Misty clouds and thrust the sad thoughts
That intrude upon my reverie far away

The wordy symbols strike my pensive memories,
Causing the indolent metaphors to withdraw
Into the caverns of my wandering mind…
I now have the world in my hand,
To mold and create in my own fashion

Memories

Ancient memories echoing
in the fissure of my soul,
telling my anxious mind
to be silent, but
my wandering soul cries out
to the fantasies inside gaudy,
painted dreams, and
ebony tears spill down the
crevices of unclothed thoughts.
Oh, to hold her once again,
to kiss away her tears,
to sit silently in her warmth… but
alas, it will never be,
for she has
departed forever, or
on the other hand…
Is it I?

The Ugly City

Not in the ugly city, but
in tranquil meadows
do we find our
way.

Seeking Him, but
never finding Him
until we discover
the gentle hills and
a healing
peace.

Man's frantic pursuits and
pernicious longings
lie far below
this verdant mountain;
in this hidden valley
one finds only a
healing
peace.

The Iron Horse

The Iron Horse, spewing
billowing steam, moves
slowly into the night;
it travels noisily as
it heads into the
far pink horizon.

The wooden platform,
burdened with iron soot,
remained silent after the
Iron Horse traveled
away, vanishing into
the darkening night.

To hear its lonely sigh,
not to hear myself,
is like listening to
the echo of a waterfall
hidden in a distant
mountain crevice.

I perceive her presence
as I smell the lilac scent
wafting from the open window,
feel her absence as the Iron Horse
leaves me alone with my thoughts...
my heart no longer feels.

The Room's Emptiness

I cloak her inside
My lonely soul,
Now she exists
Only in my mind,
My yesterday's love,
Now pale, now cold

In the invisible rays
Of the moonless night,
The clock strikes
Stridently, angrily
In the wee hours
Of the morn

In the coldness of
My nightmares,
In my mind's seclusion,
I listen to the
Emptiness of the
Lilac-scented room.

Then I watch as her
Image departs
Into the haze of
The unforgiving
Night, and
Silently weep

Tears Added to the Brine

Blurry memories and aging images,
Hazy dreams of warm, sandy shores
Where warm waters and sunbeams
Illuminated a private place to escape
The judgment of malicious people;
Yesterday – how far away – so untouchable.

Dreaming along past mist-covered paths,
I saw a man sitting alone on the sand;
He was throwing salt water into the sea,
His mind was confused, his eyes dark,
His presence filled my mind with melancholy,
My tears of sadness added to the ocean's brine.

I escaped to another time in my past
And saw a man sitting on rotting kelp,
Spinning a cloak from rivulets of sorrow;
His mind was blank, his eyes ashen,
His presence filled my mind with anxiety,
My tears of dread added to the ocean's brine.

I fled to another time in my past,
I saw an obese man sitting on an emerald mound
Stealing colorful gemstones from the sea;
His mind was blank, his eyes dark green,
His presence filled my mind with loathing,
My tears of disgust added to the ocean's brine.

I saw myself hiding in a sandstone cave,
Pulling vestiges of life from the damp hollows;
I discovered the first man was depression,
The second man was madness, and
The third man was self-indulgence.
In the dim loneliness of the cave, I found
I was trying to elude the absurdities of life.

Shadowy Winter Thoughts

Blood-colored water flows
inward;
shards of colored,
splintered glass
sever my
banal thoughts.

My abandoned heart
cries out
amidst the furor
of finite time,
salty beads stream down
my ashen cheeks.

Icy, lonely, rushing
tears
carve deep crimson channels
in my dreams,
leaving only ebony tendrils
of sadness.

I am alone among people,
cheerless amongst
happiness,
my grief as sharp
as needles.

My ideas fail to form
sentences,
my words fail to create
logical meanings,
my paragraphs
fall from the page.

I am no longer
a knowing poet,
only a frail,
common old man
without
answers to mankind's
long suffering.

In Fallow Meadows

In fallow meadows,
Few flowers grow
Under barren Oaks;
Row upon row,
They stand majestically,
Straining to reach the sky, as
Blue birds cackle stridently
While they fly, and
Scarce can be heard
The bullfrogs
Below.

The streams have
Meandered high and low
As the seasons go from
Cold white to sunny glow;
We, in our last years,
Will also meander and die
In the fallow meadows
Of our
Time.

In our youth, we
Capered to and fro,
With tender hearts
And voices low,
Our love – ours
To hold up high –
Tried to capture time
Before we lie
In shallow graves
In the earth below,
In the fallow meadows
Of our
Time.

The Soldier's Thoughts

Sitting on driftwood alongside an alien sea,
He wrote deep thoughts upon his wounded knee.
As the ocean murmured its sad song like a dove,
Amid the scarlet sandy dunes, soft as a glove,
He dreamt of purposes vast and high, and
The pulse of his yearning stirred the mighty sky.

The tide's cadence prodded him to write a poem,
As his wandering mind continued to roam; He wrote
The world is not able to heal from within, and
Men seem unable to exist without war's sin –
He supposed because it was their failure to fly, and
The pulse of his yearning stirred the mighty sky.

Yet, in his hopeful heart that longs for peace,
He will forever search for war's quick decrease,
Therefore, in his poem he will write a true story
Of a man who dutifully died for his country and glory, and
For whom death came silently without a sigh, and
The pulse of his yearning stirred the mighty sky.

Santa Ynez River

I love

The sound of rushing water
Flowing
> Over ancient pebbles
In a mountain stream
Shaped by a thousand seasons

I thrill

To nature's symphony
Created by
Soft Breezes
Singing songs through huge
Pine trees

I marvel

At the ballet of oak leaves
Swaying like green-clad pixies
Dancing with
> unruffled glee

Sounds of Hope

Loneliness leaves as thoughts ascend
Like sparrow hawks into the sky,
Soaring like strident winds
From tall oaks in a glade,
Pouring forth memories
Which the murmuring of
Longing souls cannot deny.
They increase in riotous turmoil
Atop wandering currents of
Time in the forlorn caverns
Of hopefulness, eventually
Exploding into golden dust.
Despair destroys happiness
Without compassion, therefore
Listen not to the lonely
Cries of anguish exploding like
Splintered glass, causing
Silver hollowed tears to fall
Like dead leaves in a forest.
Heed only the sounds of hope
That create a peaceful
Stillness in your aching
Soul.

I'm Going to the River... In My Mind

I plan to see the old moss-covered
Boulders sitting in the lazy river, and
That old scarred rainbow trout that
I tried to catch a hundred times.

I plan to sit under that old white-barked
Sycamore tree amidst gaudy yellow flowers,
Soft green ferns, and bluebells.

I plan to write poems, listen to
Taylor, Dylan, Miles, Ella, Karen, and
Carol on the radio, and watch clouds
Languidly form into white puffs above the hills.

I plan to drift back into my memories of
A time when my hair was still blond,
My body firm and tan, and my mind
Able to remember names and places.

I plan to use rhymes to remember my
Auburn-haired love, while I listen to the
Soft gurgling of the Indolent stream where
Bullfrogs croak their love songs in bass.

I plan to soak up the sun on my shoulders,
Breathe in the smell of the sage living in the
Cracks of the gold-colored shale.

I plan to listen to blue jays and acorn
Woodpeckers squawking in the
Distance, and watch sparrows jumping
From limb to limb catching butterflies.

Moreover, someday I plan to go there again
For real... just one more time, to keep all those
Wonderful memories fresh in my mind.

I Marvel About Life

I devour the rocks that lie
Beneath my wandering feet,
The bushes with red flowers
That line the hungry brook,
Then I digest nouns, verbs, and
Prepositions that paint the
Landscape with edible poems.
I listen to the rumbling earth, the
Gurgling of rushing water that consumes
Its stony bed, and the Birch tree that
Sings leafy ballads, while
Blue birds fly upside down in the
Morning currents of orange air.
Then I taste the green-rice thoughts
Which blow in from the east, and
The petals that cover warty frogs hiding in
The lotus leaves in a torpid pond, and
I sit and marvel about life.

Twilight Time

In the twilight hours at the day's end,
When the sun's rays no longer bend and
The soundless shadows of the trees
Hide beneath the curling breeze,
My night dreams start to wander
As I sit in silence and take time to ponder.
The final daylight hours soon will die
Under the clouds in a fair night's sky, then
It will be time for the frogs to sing with
Their baritone and deep bass ring, and
The dove's final cooing will start to fade.
I will then listen to An Ode to the Piano,
So very dear, as the night's mute
Darkness hides the shade, and I
Will take pleasure in the black and
White notes that drift quietly into my ear.

Ancient Rhythms

Previously Published Poetry Credits

1. Ancient Rhythms (Long Story Short)
2. Curative Rhythms (Poemepoetry)
3. The Night Frog (Poetic Diversity)
4. Moonlight Sonata (Emerge Literary Journal)
5. The Glass Pond (Poetry Breakfast)
6. The Ring Necked Dove (Wilderness House review)
7. Sleep Calmly My Child (Autumn Sound)
8. Precious Times (WestWard Quarterly)
10. The Mocking Bird (Vox Poetica)
12. Inside the Apse (welcome to wherever)
13. I Calmly Wend My Carefree Way (Penwood Review)
14. The Evening's Soft Glow (Tower Journal)
15. His Healing Balm (Westward Quarterly)
16. My Serenity (Long Story Short)
17. Summer has Arrived (Wilderness House Review)
18. A Special Summer Day (Wilderness House Review)
19. Warm Soft Summer Winds (Vox Poetica)
20. Warm Night Breezes (Wilderness House Review)
21. Time Passes Too Quickly (Autumn Sound)
22. The Placid Pond (Wilderness House Review)
23. Thoughts on the beach (Phati'tude Literary Magazine)
24 The Ocean's Tide (The Autumn Sound Review)
25. The Briny Sea (Viral Cat)
26. Time by a Lazy Flowing Brook (Autumn Sound)
27. A Wintry Rill (Wilderness House Review)
28. Winter at the Farm (Vox Poetica)
29. January Days (Word Catalyst Magazine)
30. Winter is Here (Long Story Short)
31. The Fading Winter (Vox Poetica)
36. A Spring Day (Long Story Short)
37. A Spring Brook (Tower Journal)
38. Spring Time (Greensilk Journal)
40. Spring Love (Tower Journal)

41. Spring at the Farm (Long Story Short)
43. Essence of Nature (Long Story Short)
44. My Soul Flows (Vox Poetica)
45. One Lovely, Pleasant Night (Long Story Short)
46. When the Evenings Are (Bumble Jacket Miscelllay)
48 Searching (Autumn Sound)
49. In Love's Sweet Garden (Kryitya: A Journal of Poetry)
50. Love Continues (Vox Poetica)
51. Love (Apollo's Lyre)
52. Let Us Forget (Long Story Short)
53. Together Our Love Grows Strong (Long Story Short)
54. The Sun So Bright Covers the Land (Greensilk Journal)
55. You and me (Apollos' Lyre)
56. A Peaceful Stillness (Wilderness House Review)
57. Figueroa Mountain (Penwood Review)
58. Visage Beatha (Long Story Short)
59. Pleasant memories (Kritya: A Journal of Poetry)
60. Music's Power (Vox Poetica)
61 Vanishing Summer Sun (Autumn Sound)
62. She is Gone (Word Catalyst Magazine)
63. Life (Word Catalyst Magazine)
64. The Poem (Tower Journal)
65. On a Mountain Top (Westward Quarterly)
66. A World to Mold (Westward Quarterly)
69 Sleep Calmly My Child (Autumn Sound)
70. The Iron Horse (Red Ochre Press)
71. The Room's Emptiness (Wilderness House Review)
72. Tears Added to the Brine (Welcome to Wherever)
73. Shadowy Winter Thoughts (Magic Cat Press)
75. The Soldier's Thoughts (Magic Cat Press)
76. Santa Ynez River (Greensilk Journal)

James G. Piatt

About the Author

Dr. Piatt earned his B.S. and M.A. from California State Polytechnic University and his doctorate from BYU. Prior to his retirement, he was a missile engineer and launch-conductor, a science teacher and alternative high school principal, a Junior College professor of psychology, engineering, and philosophy, as well as Dean. He was also a College Professor of Education and an administrator of Master of Education programs. He has published over 490 poems, 31 short stories, and seven essays in over 60 magazines and anthologies.

Broken Publications published his debut book of poetry *The Silent Pond* in 2012. Write Words Inc. published his debut science fiction novel *The Ideal Society* in 2012. *The Monk* was published by Broken Publications in 2013 and *The Nostradamus Prophecies* will be released later in 2014.